W9-CGP-235

Cruisers

by Michael Green

Content Consultant:
Jack A. Green, Historian
Naval Historical Center

C A P S T O N E   P R E S S

M A N K A T O ,   M I N N E S O T A

C A P S T O N E   P R E S S

818 North Willow Street • Mankato, Minnesota 56001
http://www.capstone-press.com

Printed in the United States of America.

Library of Congress Cataloging-in-Publication Data
Green, Michael, 1952-
    Cruisers/by Michael Green.
    p. cm. -- (Land and sea)
    Includes bibliographical references and index.
    Summary: An introduction to history, purpose, operation, weaponry, and
more of the medium-sized warships known for their speed and long-range
cruising ability.
    ISBN 1-56065-556-9
    1. Cruisers (Warships)--United States--Juvenile literature. [1. Cruisers
(Warships) 2. Warships.] I. Title. II. Series: Land and sea (Mankato, Minn.)

V820.3.G74 1998
623.8'253--dc21

                                                    97-7756
                                                     CIP
                                                     AC

Editorial credits
Editor, Timothy Larson; Cover design, Timothy Halldin; Illustrations,
    James Franklin; Photo Research Assistant, Michelle L. Norstad
Photo credits
Archive Photos, 16, 20
U.S. Navy, cover, 4, 6, 9, 10, 12, 15, 18, 23, 24, 26, 28, 30, 33, 34, 36, 38
    40, 47

Table of Contents

Chapter 1

Cruisers

Cruisers are medium-sized warships. Cruise means to move quickly and easily. A warship is a ship with guns and other weapons that navies use for war. Navies named these ships cruisers for their speed and ease of movement. Cruisers are useful for many military jobs because of their speed and weapons.

One of a cruiser's most important jobs is protecting aircraft carriers during battle. An aircraft carrier is a large warship that carries planes. Cruisers protect aircraft carriers as part of battle groups. A battle group is made up of aircraft carriers plus support ships and planes. Support means helper.

Cruisers protect aircraft carriers from enemy ships, planes, and submarines. A submarine is a ship that can travel both on top of water and underwater. Navies also use cruisers to attack enemy ships and targets on land.

Cruisers are medium-sized warships that move quickly and easily.

The captain and sailors control a cruiser from the bridge.

Before 1912, the U.S. Navy named most new cruisers after states. The navy also named some cruisers after people. From 1912 to 1962, the navy named cruisers after cities and U.S. territories. Since 1962, the navy has named cruisers after states, cities, and people.

The U.S. Navy puts cruisers that are alike into groups called classes. The navy names each class after the first ship in the group. Sometimes, a class has only one ship in it.

The navy often creates new classes for each kind of cruiser it commissions. A commission is a navy order to put a ship into service. Some older cruisers change classes when the navy improves them.

Cruiser Form

All cruisers have the same basic form. They have many of the same features as other ships. They have an anchor in the bow. The bow is the front of a ship. Propellers called screws are located in the stern. The stern is the rear of a ship. Screws push cruisers through water.

Cruisers are divided into decks. The first deck is the top deck. It is the top deck that people can see from outside. Sailors call the top deck, topside. The other decks lie below the top deck. Sailors call the lower decks, below.

A control tower called a superstructure is located on the top deck. The superstructure has a room called the bridge. The bridge is where the captain and sailors control the ship. The superstructure also holds a cruiser's radar. Radar is a type of machinery that uses radio waves to locate and guide things. A cruiser's guns are located on the top deck, too.

The lower decks have many rooms called compartments. Some compartments are for sleeping. Some are for cooking and eating. Some compartments are for meetings. Other compartments make up a small hospital for sailors who are hurt.

A cruiser's boilers and turbines are in compartments called engine rooms. A boiler is a special kind of heater. It makes steam to power a turbine. A turbine is an engine. A turbine turns a cruiser's screws. Several turbines operate together to make cruisers move at high speeds. They also help cruisers travel over long distances.

Size, Weight, Speed, and Distance

Cruisers are smaller than large warships like aircraft carriers and battleships. Cruisers have smaller guns and thinner armor than large warships. Armor is a protective covering of metal.

Displacement describes the weight of ships. Displacement is the weight of the water that a ship pushes away from itself while afloat. A ship's displacement changes depending on the load it carries.

The smallest U.S. Navy cruisers displaced about 3,750 tons (3,375 metric tons) of water.

Cruisers move quickly through the water because of the power of their turbine engines.

The largest U.S. Navy cruisers displaced 27,500 tons (24,750 metric tons) of water. Today's navy cruisers have an average displacement of 9,600 tons (8,640 metric tons) of water.

People measure the speed of ships and boats in knots. One knot is 1.15 miles per hour. The fastest navy cruisers can reach top speeds of 35 knots. This is about 40 miles (64 kilometers) per hour.

Chapter 2

Cruiser Weapons

The U.S. Navy has armed its cruisers with guns, missiles, and torpedoes. A missile is an explosive that uses a rocket to fly long distances. A torpedo is an explosive that travels under water.

The navy armed its early cruisers with guns and torpedoes. Later cruisers had guns and missiles or just missiles. Many of today's cruisers have guns, missiles, and torpedoes.

Main and Secondary Batteries

The navy groups guns on warships by their size and use. The size of some guns is given in inches. The size of other guns is given in millimeters. The inches or millimeters tell you the inside width of a gun barrel.

Today's cruisers have missiles, as well as guns and torpedoes.

The navy mounted guns on early cruisers in turrets.

Guns that have the same size and use are placed in a set. Each set is called a battery. Sailors control and fire each battery of guns as a group. This way sailors can fire many guns at one target.

Navy cruisers built before the early 1940s had two main gun sizes. One group had large guns. The large guns made up a battery called the main battery. Sailors used the main battery to shoot at enemy ships and targets on land.

The main battery guns were mounted in large turrets. A turret is an armored gun shelter. Turrets allow ships to shoot at targets more quickly and easily. Turrets can turn from side to side. They also can raise guns up and down. The navy still mounts warship guns in turrets.

Early cruisers also had a battery of smaller guns. This battery was called the secondary battery. Many secondary battery guns also were mounted in turrets. Some were mounted into the hull. Sailors used the secondary battery to fire only at enemy ships. The guns in the secondary battery were not large enough to hit targets on land.

Dual-Purpose and Antiaircraft Guns

By the early 1940s, the U.S. Navy saw that its secondary guns were not very useful. The navy replaced the secondary batteries on its cruisers with dual-purpose guns. Dual means double or two. Dual-purpose guns were more useful. They could fire at ships and at other targets.

The navy grouped dual-purpose guns into batteries. Each dual-purpose battery had two five-inch guns mounted together in turrets. A crew of 14 sailors operated these turrets. A well-trained gun crew could fire up to 22 rounds per minute. A round is a bullet or shell.

The navy also fitted these cruisers with antiaircraft gun batteries. Antiaircraft guns are used to defend against attacking planes. These guns are automatic. This means they can fire on their own. Once fired, these guns keep firing until they run out of rounds or sailors stop them.

Torpedoes and Missiles

Until 1934, most U.S. Navy cruisers carried torpedoes. Sailors shot the torpedoes from tubes built into the ship. Between 1934 and 1936, the navy removed torpedoes from its cruisers. The navy felt that torpedoes were more useful weapons for planes, submarines, and destroyers. A destroyer is a small warship used for hunting submarines.

By 1955, the navy started replacing cruiser guns with missiles. Missiles can travel farther than gun shells. This means that missiles can hit targets farther away than guns can.

Radar

Radar was an important invention to U.S. Navy warships. Before radar, sailors aimed ship guns at targets using eyesight and optics. Optics are tools

All U.S. Navy cruisers have had radar since 1942.

that magnify faraway objects. A telescope is an example of an optic tool.

Radar shows where things are located much better than eyesight and optics. It works in most weather and battle conditions. It also works over long distances. These features helped warships spot enemy targets more easily and aim their weapons better.

Navy scientists were leaders in using radar on warships. By the end of 1942, many navy warships had radar systems. Today, all warships have radar systems.

Chapter 3

Early Cruiser History

The U.S. Navy did not have many cruisers until the late 1800s. The navy relied mainly on battleships. But in 1904, the navy changed its mind and began building new cruisers. Since then, the navy has built many cruisers and created many cruiser classes.

The navy first commissioned four cruisers. These new cruisers were known as the Tennessee class. Each ship had a displacement of 14,500 tons (13,050 metric tons) of water. Tennessee class cruisers had an average speed of 22 knots. Each of these cruisers carried 900 sailors.

The navy commissioned the Chester class cruisers in 1908. Chester class cruisers were

The *Chester* was the first cruiser the U.S. Navy commissioned for the Chester class.

17

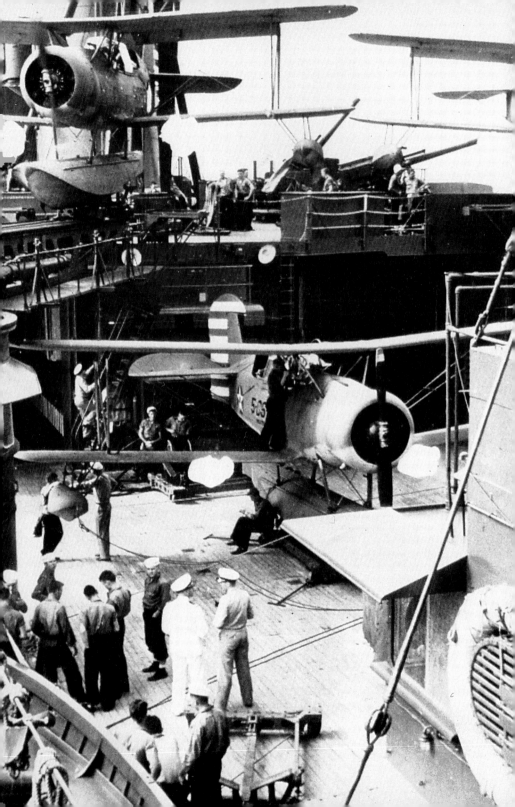

smaller than the Tennessee class cruisers. Chester class cruisers had an average displacement of 3,750 tons (3,375 metric tons) of water. They each had a top speed of 22 knots. They carried 560 sailors. The navy used these ships through the 1920s.

Omaha Class Cruisers

During the 1920s, the navy began building the Omaha class cruisers. These cruisers were also smaller than the Tennessee class cruisers but larger than Chester class cruisers. They were much faster than the older cruisers. Omaha class cruisers could reach a top speed of 35 knots. The average displacement of these ships was 9,507 tons (8,556 metric tons) of water.

The Omaha class cruisers carried crews of 458 sailors. They also carried seaplanes to scout for the enemy. A seaplane is a plane that can float on the water. The planes took off from small runways on the cruisers' top decks.

Although the Omaha class cruisers were fast, the navy saw that these cruisers had problems. Their guns were not as powerful as those on cruisers in other navies. Omaha class cruisers also handled

Omaha class cruisers carried seaplanes for scouting.

The *Alaska* was one of two U.S. Navy large cruisers.

poorly in rough seas. After building these cruisers, the navy made many attempts to build the ideal cruiser. The navy wanted a cruiser with the best size and speed.

World War II-Era Cruisers
The navy decided to build new classes of cruisers in the early 1930s. The navy used these cruisers

along with the older Omaha class cruisers during World War II (1939-1945).

The U.S. Navy grouped the new cruiser classes into three general types. The navy called them large cruisers, heavy cruisers, and light cruisers. Seven heavy cruisers and three light cruisers sank during World War II.

The term large cruiser refers to the ship's size. Large cruisers were almost twice as big as the Omaha class cruisers. In fact, they were about the same size as some battleships.

The terms light and heavy cruiser have nothing to do with the weight of the ships. They refer to the size of the guns carried on the cruisers. U.S. Navy heavy cruisers had eight-inch, heavy guns. Light cruisers had six-inch, light guns.

Large Cruisers

In 1944, the U.S. Navy commissioned only two large cruisers. The ships were named the *Alaska* and the *Guam*. Both cruisers were 808 feet (242 meters) long. The ships were in the Alaska class.

The *Alaska* and the *Guam* displaced 27,500 tons (24,750 metric tons) of water. They were powered by steam turbine engines and each had a top speed of 33 knots. Crews of 2,251 sailors operated these ships.

These ships were expensive for the navy to operate because of their size. Advances in cruiser hull forms and weapons made these ships obsolete. Obsolete means out-of-date. The navy stopped using large cruisers in 1947.

Heavy Cruisers

When the United States entered World War II in 1941, the navy had 18 heavy cruisers in service. Most of them carried heavy guns and other smaller guns.

Forty percent of the navy's heavy cruisers were in the New Orleans class. There were seven ships in the class. These cruisers were powered by steam turbine engines. They each had a top speed of about 33 knots. Each ship in this class carried crews of 366 sailors. They also carried four seaplanes for scouting.

In July 1944, a new class with 17 heavy cruisers entered service. These ships belonged to the Baltimore class. They displaced about 13,000

Heavy cruisers had heavy guns.

tons (11,700 metric tons) of water. They had a top speed of 33 knots. Each ship had nine eight-inch guns, and 12 five-inch guns. The Baltimore class heavy cruisers carried as many as 1,700 sailors each.

Light Cruisers

The U.S. Navy entered World War II with 19 light cruisers in service. The navy needed more

Light cruisers had light guns.

aircraft carriers soon after the war started. It
changed nine light cruisers into aircraft carriers.
Three of these light cruisers sank early in the war.
The navy ordered another 40 light cruisers during
the war.

There were two main light cruiser classes. The
first was called the Atlanta class. There were

eight ships in this class. Steam turbine engines powered these ships to a top speed of 40 knots. The Atlanta class cruisers each displaced 6,000 tons (5,400 metric tons) of water. Crews of 800 sailors ran each ship.

The navy armed the Atlanta class cruisers with 16 five-inch guns. The guns were mounted in pairs. The guns could be used against enemy planes and ships. Atlanta class cruisers also had many smaller antiaircraft guns. These cruisers were also known as antiaircraft cruisers. This was because they carried so many antiaircraft guns.

The other class of light cruisers was the Cleveland class. The navy built more than 30 ships for this class. The Cleveland class cruisers each displaced 13,600 tons (12,240 metric tons) of water. They were run by crews of 992 to 1,200 sailors.

The cruisers in this class had 12 six-inch guns. The navy arranged the guns in groups of three in turrets. Cleveland class cruisers also had six pairs of lighter guns. The navy mounted them in turrets, too.

Chapter 4

Recent Cruiser History

At the end of World War II, the U.S. Navy had the largest fleet of warships in the world. A fleet is a group of warships under one command. Most of their cruisers were worn out. The navy decided that its cruisers needed to be updated.

Between 1955 and 1958, the navy changed some of its heavy cruisers into guided-missile cruisers. A guided missile is a missile that is guided by radar to its target. The world's first guided-missile cruisers were the *Albany*, the *Chicago*, and the *Columbus*. These cruisers were in the Albany class.

The navy uses guided missiles against many targets. Some of these targets are enemy planes

The *Canberra* was one of the cruisers that the navy changed into guided-missile cruisers.

The U.S. Navy's first guided-missile cruisers had top speeds of 30 knots.

and ships. The navy also uses guided missiles to shoot down enemy missiles.

The early navy missiles and radar systems were very large. The navy decided that cruisers were best suited for these systems. Only cruisers could carry both the missiles and their radar systems. Battleships did not have room for them because they carried so many guns. Other warships were too small.

The navy's first guided-missile cruisers were powered by steam turbine engines. Their top speed was limited to about 30 knots. They also needed refueling every few days.

Engine Problems

The U.S. Navy recognized that the limited speed of the first guided-missile cruisers was a problem. The navy also saw that refueling them so often was a problem.

While the navy was changing to guided-missile cruisers, it was also experimenting with a new kind of turbine engine. The engine was nuclear powered. Nuclear power is a powerful kind of energy that lasts longer than other kinds of energy. The fuel for these engines is nuclear rods. Rods are nuclear-charged metal bars.

The navy wanted to put nuclear-powered turbine engines in its new aircraft carriers. Tests showed that nuclear-powered aircraft carriers could have a top speed of more than 35 knots. The navy also believed it would only have to refuel nuclear-powered aircraft carriers every 15 years.

The navy knew that cruisers would slow down nuclear-powered aircraft carriers. This was

The *Long Beach* was the U.S. Navy's first nuclear-powered cruiser.

because the cruisers' would need fuel more often than the carriers. The cruisers' refueling needs also would keep them from scouting ahead of the new aircraft carriers. The navy knew it needed to build nuclear-powered, guided-missile cruisers.

The *Long Beach*

The U.S. Navy started working on a nuclear-powered cruiser during the mid-1950s. The navy commissioned the first nuclear-powered cruiser in 1961. The cruiser was the *Long Beach*. It was a guided-missile test cruiser. The navy built the *Long*

Beach to try out new machines, missiles, guns, and nuclear-powered engines.

The *Long Beach* had a top speed of 31 knots. Compared to the first guided-missile cruisers, the *Long Beach* was a little faster. It did not have to refuel as often because of its nuclear-powered engines. But its engine was still not as fast as the engines in nuclear-powered aircraft carriers.

When the navy first built the *Long Beach*, it had no guns on it. It only had different types of missiles. The ship could use its missiles against planes, ships, and submarines. The *Long Beach* also could use its missiles against targets on land.

In the late 1970s, the navy decided to add guns to the *Long Beach*. Two five-inch guns were mounted on the ship's top deck. The navy added the guns for defense against enemy planes and boats. The guns protected the ship while it fired its missiles at other targets.

The tests with the *Long Beach* helped the navy. The tests showed that guided-missile cruisers could still protect aircraft carriers. Their guided missiles could hit targets very far away. Their radar could easily spot enemy ships and planes. These features helped make up for the cruisers' slower speeds.

Modern U.S. Navy Cruisers

Between 1960 and 1970, the navy built 21 new guided-missile cruisers. During that time, the navy realized that nuclear-powered cruisers were expensive to build and operate. Only the *Bainbridge*, the *California*, and the *South Carolina* were nuclear powered.

Starting in 1972, the navy began building four new cruisers. These guided-missile cruisers were the Virginia class. They all were nuclear powered and had a top speed of 30 or more knots. Each ship displaced about 11,000 tons (9,900 metric tons) of water. They measured 585 feet long (176 meters). Crews of 530 sailors ran these ships.

The missiles on these cruisers could be used against air, sea, and land targets. Other Virginia class weapons included guns and attack helicopters. A helicopter is an aircraft with rotating blades on top. Helicopters can take off and land in small areas. The navy put guns and missiles on these helicopters, too.

Today, most of the cruisers the navy built between 1960s and 1970s are still in service. The

Today's U.S. Navy cruisers have guns and missiles.

navy plans to remove these cruisers from service. The navy will remove the nuclear-powered cruisers as they need to be refueled.

The U.S. Navy's Newest Cruisers

Starting in 1980, the U.S. Navy began building Ticonderoga class cruisers. More than 27 ships are in the Ticonderoga class. The Ticonderoga class cruisers each displace 9,600 tons (8,640

Ticonderoga class cruisers have two 20mm guns.

metric tons) of water. They carry crews of 353 sailors. The navy still uses Ticonderoga class cruisers.

These ships are not nuclear powered. They have a new type of gas turbine engine. The gas turbine engine produces a lot of power. With four of these engines, Ticonderoga class cruisers can reach top speeds of 35 knots. This makes them as fast as the nuclear-powered aircraft carriers.

These engines do have to be refueled more often than the nuclear-powered engines. But the new gas turbine engines are cheaper to operate than nuclear-powered engines. The navy feels that the engines' operating cost and power make up for their refueling problem.

Ticonderoga Class Weapons

The strength of the Ticonderoga class cruisers is their Aegis air defense systems. The Aegis is a computer-controlled radar system. It can track more than 100 targets at the same time. It can also guide 10 missiles to their targets at the same time.

The navy armed Ticonderoga class cruisers with Tomahawk cruise missiles. A cruise missile is an advanced guided missile. A cruise missile has an on-board computer. This computer helps guide the missile towards a target. Cruisers launch Tomahawk cruise missiles mainly at targets on land.

Ticonderoga class cruisers also have two types of guns. The first is the five-inch, lightweight gun. This gun is automatic. It can fire 16 to 20 rounds per minute. The ships have two 20mm, computer-controlled guns, too.

These cruisers have other missiles for attacking enemy ships and planes. Many cruisers also carry one antisubmarine helicopter. An antisubmarine helicopter attacks enemy submarines.

Missile Launcher

Radar

Helicopter Pad

The *Ticonderoga*

Bridge

Radar

Missile Launcher

Light Gun

47

Chapter 5

Safety and the Future

In the past, cruisers used their speed to protect themselves from the enemy. Speed helped cruisers avoid enemy attacks. Moving quickly, cruisers could move away from slower ships. Cruisers' speeds also made it hard for enemy weapons to hit them.

Many of today's cruisers are fast. But being able to move fast cannot always protect a cruiser. Slower ships now use missiles to attack ships that are far away. Jet planes also can attack ships easily.

Modern navy cruisers rely more on their radar systems than speed. Radar systems can warn cruisers that enemy ships, planes, or missiles are coming. This gives them time to move out of the way. Radar also gives cruisers time to prepare their weapons for defense.

Sailors use radar systems to watch for enemy ships, planes, and missiles.

Sailors learn how to fight fires.

Other Safety Concerns

The navy teaches sailors that safety is very important. Emergencies like enemy attacks and accidents can cause a lot of harm to ships. An emergency is a sudden and unsafe situation. Sailors on cruisers learn they have jobs to do in an emergency. The navy teaches them how to fight fires and repair damage. This type of work is called damage control.

Every sailor on a cruiser has a life jacket. A life jacket helps people float in water. Sailors wear their life jackets during battle. They also wear life jackets when the sea is rough.

When sailors are on the top deck of a cruiser, they wear helmets. The helmets protect their heads from bullets.

The fuel that powers today's U.S. Navy nuclear cruisers has to be handled very carefully. New and used nuclear rods are harmful to humans. Sailors must handle the rods very carefully. Sailors also have to store the rods in special containers.

The Future of Cruisers

New weapons present safety problems for U.S. Navy cruisers. Many powerful kinds of missiles now exist around the world. Cruisers cannot defend themselves or aircraft carriers against all the new missiles. Some military officials say there is no longer a need for warships like cruisers.

To remain valuable, newer and safer cruisers will have to be built in the future. The navy will have to make changes in cruiser size and cruiser radar protection. Most importantly, tomorrow's cruisers will have to be able to defend against modern weapons.

Words to Know

armor (AR-mur)—a protective metal covering

battery (BAT-uh-ree)—a group of guns that are alike

boiler (BOI-lur)—a special heater that makes steam to power turbines

bridge (BRIJ)—the room where the captain controls a ship

commission (kuh-MISH-uhn)—a navy order to put a ship into service

cruise missile (KROOZ MISS-uhl)—a type of missile that steers itself to a target using an on-board computer

destroyer (di-STROI-ur)—a small warship used for hunting submarines

dual (DOO-uhl)—double or two

fire control (FIRE kuhn-TROHL)—the method of aiming weapons at a target

fleet (FLEET)—a group of warships under one command

helicopter (HEL-uh-kop-tur)—an aircraft with rotating blades on top

hull (HUHL)—the body of a ship

knot (NOT)—a measurement of speed for ships and boats; 1.15 miles per hour

missile (MISS-uhl)—an explosive that flies long distances

nuclear power (NOO-klee-ur POU-ur)—a powerful kind of energy that lasts longer than other kinds of energy

optics (OP-tiks)—tools that magnify faraway objects

radar (RAY-dar)—machinery that uses radio waves to locate and guide things

seaplane (SEE-plane)—a plane that can float on the water

submarine (SUHB-muh-reen)—a ship that can travel both on top of water and underwater

torpedo (tor-PEE-doh)—an explosive that travels underwater

turbine (TUR-bine)—an engine powered by steam, water, or gas

turret (TUR-it)—an armored shelter for guns

To Learn More

Asimov, Isaac and Elizabeth Kaplan. *How Do Big Ships Float?* Milwaukee: Gareth Stevens, 1993.

Bailey, Dennis M. *Aegis Guided Missile Cruiser.* Osceola, Wis.: Motorbooks International, 1991.

Friedman, Norman. *U.S. Cruisers: An Illustrated Design History*. Annapolis, Md.: Naval Institute Press, 1984.

Preston, Antony. *Cruisers: An Illustrated History, 1880-1980*. London: Bison Books, 1980.

Useful Addresses

Naval Historical Center
Washington Navy Yard
901 M Street SE
Washington, DC 20374-5060

U.S. Navy Cruiser *Little Rock*
Buffalo Naval And Servicemen's Park
One Naval Park Cove
Buffalo, NY 14202

U.S. Navy Cruiser *Olympia* Association
Penn's Landing
Delaware Avenue and Spruce Street
Philadelphia, PA 19106

Internet Sites

Guided Missiles
http://www.nawcwpns.navy.mil:80/clmf/bat.html

Navy: Welcome Aboard
http://www.navy.mil/

U.S. Cruiser Lists
http://www.membrane.com:80/~elmer/
  navy/cruisers

U.S. Navy History
http://www.history.navy.mil/

Ticonderoga class cruisers carry missiles.

Index